Ahead of Their Time

A great college football team stands up for fairness, equality, and teammates.

By Eric Golanty

1951 Undefeated - University of San Francisco Dons

Boyd 1951

When I discovered the inspirational story of the 1951 University of San Francisco Dons football team -- what some people refer to as "the best team you never heard of" -- I wanted to share it with kids, parents, and teachers so they could be reminded that sports participation can mean a lot more than getting whatever you can for yourself. Notwithstanding their prowess on the football field, the true greatness of the '51 Dons is their honor, integrity, and esprit de corps.

I owe much to Kristine Clark's book about the team, *Undefeated, Untied, and Uninvited.* I am indebted to all who supported me in this endeavor.

~Eric Golanty

Project Web Site

http://www.ergo84.com/51dons.htm

- Find links to helpful resources
- Explore classroom activities
- Order books
- Contact Eric Golanty

Book design: Tamsen Bryon

ISBN: 978-0-9842644-0-7

1951 Undefeated - University of San Francisco Dons

This story is about a group of honorable young men who played on a college football team back in 1951. That team was the University of San Francisco Dons.

Dons is the University of San Francisco's mascot. It's a Spanish word used to signify a man worthy of respect.

More about...
Mascots
on page 31.

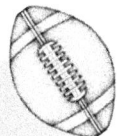

On the field the Dons were great. However, that is only part of the reason to tell this story. More important is that the Dons showed the whole world -- back then and even now -- that there's a lot more to sports than just winning.

Here's what happened...

More about...
Football Helmets
on page 32.

In the 1951 college football season, the Dons won all of their games. They defeated their opponents by an average score of 33-8. Among the hundreds of American college football teams, the Dons were:

#1 in rushing defense

#3 in total defense

#8 in total offense

#9 in total yards rushing

#14 overall

More about...
Rushing
on page 34.

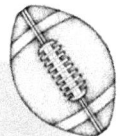

Ollie Matson

Ollie Matson, the Dons fullback, was one of the top players in the United States. He was voted All America, an honor given only to the very best college football players. He also was ninth in the voting for the Heisman Trophy, which is awarded each year to the most outstanding player in college football.

More about...
The Heisman Trophy
on page 36.

Besides Ollie Matson, the 1951 Dons had many other talented players. After college, ten members of the team were chosen to play professional football in the National Football League (NFL). Five of that group played in the NFL Pro Bowl. This means they were voted the best at their positions by other professional football players, professional football coaches, and football fans.

Three players from the '51 Dons team who went on to play professional football -- Gino Marchetti, Ollie Matson, and Bob St. Clair -- were chosen to be in the NFL Hall of Fame. That means they are among the best ever to play football. No other college team in American history has placed three players in the NFL Hall of Fame.

More about...
The NFL Hall of Fame
on page 37.

The 1951 University of San Francisco Dons may have been one of the best college teams ever. Unfortunately, however, the team didn't get a chance to prove it.

The way sports teams show how good they are is to play well against other good teams. In 1951, the USF Dons football team had trouble doing that because many other strong teams refused to play them; they were afraid they'd lose. In the 1951 season, the Dons could find only eight opponents; one team they played twice!

How frustrating it must have been for the '51 Dons players not to get the chance to compete at the highest level and to measure themselves against strong competitors.

When the 1951 regular football season ended, the Dons' only chance to show what they could do against top-notch competition was to play in a bowl game.

Bowl games take place after the regular football season ends. Good teams are invited to play in them and people pay money to watch. The more exciting and interesting a bowl game is, the more money the bowl game organizers can make.

The first college bowl game in America was the Rose Bowl, played on January 1, 1902, between the University of Michigan and Stanford University (Michigan won, 49-0).

For many years, the Rose Bowl was the only postseason bowl game between two college teams. Now, nearly 40 bowl games are played each year around New Year's Day.

Miami Orange Bowl

In November of 1951, the Orange Bowl Organization invited the Georgia Tech University Yellow Jackets to play in the Orange Bowl Game on New Year's Day, 1952. Georgia Tech had won all of its games during the 1951 season and was ranked Number 5 in the United States. Eleven teams were being considered for Georgia Tech's opponent, including the Dons!

12

To play Georgia Tech in the Orange Bowl was just what the Dons needed. They could find out just how good they were, and if they measured up to what they believed about themselves, they would show others, too.

Eventually, the Orange Bowl Organization made its decision: The Dons were invited to play Georgia Tech in the Orange Bowl game. As soon as they found this out, the Dons players and all of their supporters were thrilled.

Except, there was a catch...

The Orange Bowl Organization told the Dons they could compete in the game only if the team's two African-American players, Burl Toler and Ollie Matson, did not participate.

'51 Dons players (left to right) Burl Toler, Ed Brown, Gino Marchetti, Ollie Matson.

This shocked and angered the Dons players, and they flatly refused to compete in the game. It didn't matter that their season would end without getting the chance to show their football talents. Ollie and Burl were teammates. All for one and one for all! There wasn't even a team meeting to discuss it. Here's what some of the Dons players said:

"Ollie and Burl were just brothers to us. It was all or nothing, that's the way we played."

~ Bob Springer, Halfback

"I wanted no part of going without them; I wanted no part of going even if they had to stay at another hotel."

~ Gino Marchetti, Defensive Tackle

"We played in Tulsa, Oklahoma in 1950. You couldn't believe what they yelled at us. I think it made us stronger. We weren't a football team, we were a football family. We didn't see black and white. We were close. There was never any question, we all go or nobody goes."

~ Ralph Thomas, Offensive End

When the Dons refused to play without *all* their players, the Orange Bowl Organization took back the team's invitation. They said that it was because the University of San Francisco was too small (only 1,200 students back then) to have many fans go to the game. They also said that the Dons hadn't played enough tough teams, so people around the United States hadn't heard of them and wouldn't come to the game.

Those weren't the only reasons. San Francisco sportscaster Ira Blue reported that all the bowls played in the southern part of the United States (the Orange Bowl in Florida, the Cotton Bowl in Texas, the Sugar Bowl in Louisiana, and the Gator Bowl in Florida) had decided not to invite teams with African-American players.

On New Year's Day, 1952, the Georgia Tech Yellow Jackets defeated the Baylor University Bears in the Orange Bowl, 17-14.

The Dons stayed home.

Why did the Orange Bowl Organization tell the Dons they could play only if their African-American teammates didn't? The reason is that they feared that white football fans would not buy tickets to see the game if African-Americans were to play.

Today we are accustomed to seeing African-Americans in college and professional sports, and it's hard to imagine an athlete not being allowed to compete because of her or his skin color, family background, or religion.

It hasn't always been this way. Because of prejudice, for many years, including 1951, most colleges would not accept African-American students, and some would not compete against college teams with African-American athletes.

More about...
***African-Americans in
College Football***
on page 38.

This was especially true in the southern part of the United States, where local laws forced African-Americans, who were referred to as "Colored," to live separately from white people. This is called *racial segregation.*

Segregated waiting room at a bus station in Durham, North Carolina, 1940.

African-Americans were not allowed to eat in the same restaurants as whites, stay in the same hotels, go to the same schools or movies, drink at the same drinking fountains, or sit on buses and trains in whichever seats they wanted.

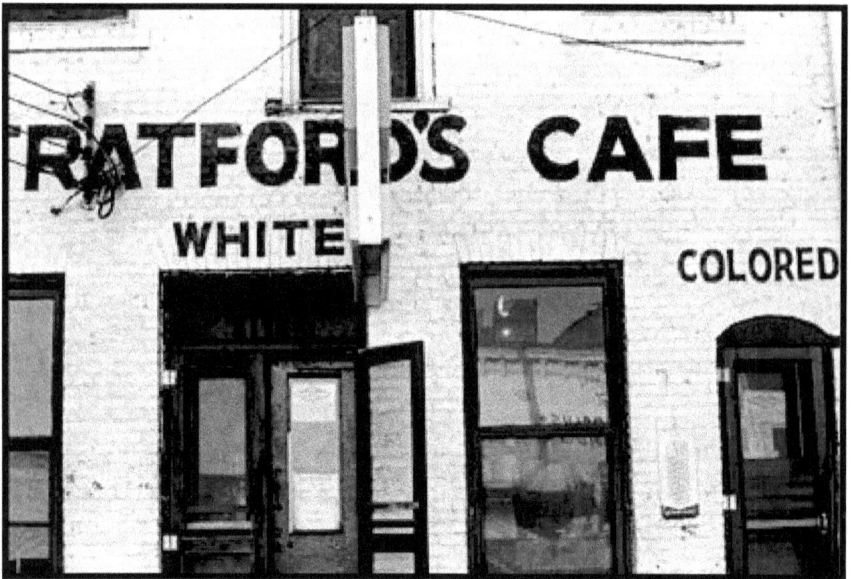

Segregated restaurant in Atlanta, Georgia.

To the Dons and their supporters, not allowing the team's African-American players to participate in the Orange Bowl was wrong. And it made no sense. African-Americans had served with valor and distinction in the armed forces during World War II between 1941 and 1945, and racial segregation was stopped in the U.S. military in 1948.

The Tuskegee Airmen were America's first all-African-American military airmen, serving with the 332nd Fighter Group during World War II. The unit was among the most highly decorated of the war.

21

Also, by 1951, after many years of not being allowed to, African-Americans were playing in major professional sports. In 1946, Kenny Washington and Woody Strode, outstanding players at UCLA, became the first African-Americans to play modern professional football. In that same year, Marion Motley and Bill Willis were hired to play for the Cleveland Browns of the NFL. Both are in the NFL Hall of Fame.

Marion Motley

Bill Willis

Jackie Robinson

In 1947, Jackie Robinson became the first African-American to play major league baseball. Before then, major league baseball did not allow African-American players.

Some people believe that in sports, winning isn't the most important thing, it's the only thing. That means not only defeating opponents but also each individual athlete doing almost anything to gain attention, fame, and perhaps a lot of money.

More about...
Making Money in
Professional Sports
on page 40.

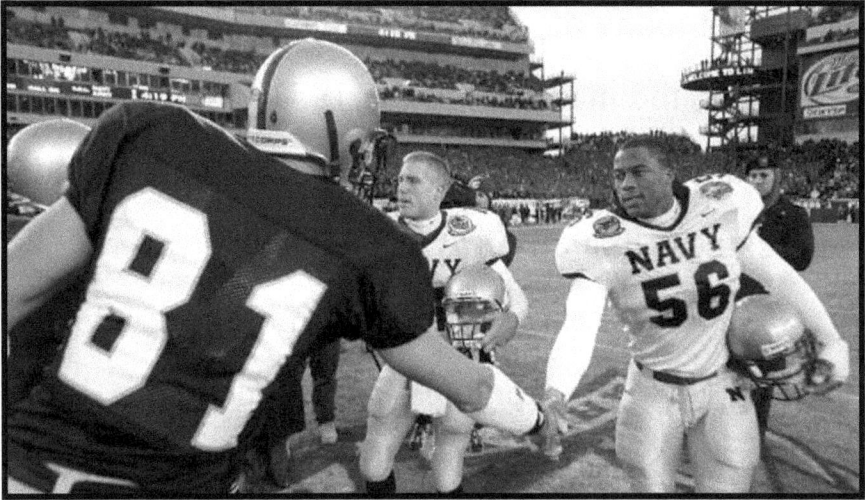

Other people believe that the best thing about playing sports is that it makes you a better person. It teaches you to work hard so you can get good at anything you choose to do, not just sports. Playing sports also teaches you to be fair, to respect your opponents, to win humbly, and to lose gracefully.

Not many of us can be great at sports. However, the members of the 1951 University of San Francisco Dons football team show us a kind of greatness that all of us can achieve.

All of us can try to do the right thing. We can support our teammates, family members, friends, and neighbors even if it means passing up an opportunity to get something we might want for ourselves.

Many years after the 1951 season, the University of San Francisco gave the team an award, called a Doctor of Humane Letters. The award said...

The men we honor today paid a price for their integrity. They refused a bowl bid rather than compromise their values. They sacrificed glory for honor and character.

Members of the 1951 USF Dons football team receiving an Honorary Doctor of Humane Letters award in 2001.

In 2001, to celebrate the 50th anniversary of its memorable season and heroic decision, the United States Senate honored the team.

SENATE RESOLUTION 346

Acknowledging that the undefeated and untied 1951 University of San Francisco Dons football team suffered a grave injustice by not being invited to any post-season Bowl game due to racial prejudice that prevailed at the time and seeking appropriate recognition for the surviving members of that championship team.

Whereas the 1951 University of San Francisco Dons football team completed its championship season with an unblemished record;

Whereas this closely knit team failed to receive an invitation to compete in any post-season Bowl game because two of its players were African-American;

Whereas the 1951 University of San Francisco Dons football team courageously and rightly rejected an offer to play in a Bowl game without their African-American teammates;

Whereas this exceptionally gifted football team, for the most objectionable of reasons, was deprived of the opportunity to prove itself before a national audience;

Whereas ten members of this team were drafted into the National Football League, five played in the Pro Bowl, and three were inducted into the Hall of Fame;

Whereas our Nation has made great strides in overcoming the barriers of oppression, intolerance, and discrimination in order to ensure fair and equal treatment for every American by every American; and

Whereas it is appropriate and fitting to now offer these athletes the attention and accolades they earned but were denied: Now, therefore, be it

Resolved, That the Senate --

(1) applauds the undefeated and untied 1951 University of San Francisco Dons football team for its determination, commitment, and integrity, both on and off the playing field; and

(2) acknowledges that the treatment endured by this team was wrong and that recognition for its accomplishments is long overdue.

In 2001, looking back 50 years, San Francisco mayor Willie Brown noted that the 1951 Dons football players were ahead of their time. They stood up for fairness and equality two years before Rosa Parks refused to give up her seat on a bus to a white man, and several years before college students from all over America demonstrated in support of racial equality.

In 1953 in Montgomery, Alabama, Rosa Parks refused to give up her seat on a bus to a white man. Back then, this was a crime, and she was arrested and put in jail. This touched off an organized struggle to gain civil rights for all African-Americans.

More about...
College Students and Racial Equality
on page 42.

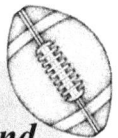

*"I have a dream
that my four little
children will one day
live in a nation where
they will not be judged
by the color of their skin
but by the content
of their character."*

~ Martin Luther King, Jr.

*"Focusing your life solely
on making a buck shows
a certain poverty of
ambition. It asks too little
of yourself. Because it's
only when you hitch your
wagon to something
larger than yourself that
you realize your true
potential."*

~ President Barack Obama

30

More About...

Mascots

A mascot is the symbol of an organization, such as a school. Your school may have a

mascot. Some mascots are animals, such as the University of Kentucky Wildcats or the University of Wisconsin Badgers.

University of San Francisco symbol

A mascot can represent something about a college's location, like the University of Miami Hurricanes. Or, a mascot can represent something special about a college, such as the Purdue University Boilermakers or the University of Notre Dame Fighting Irish.

Some mascots are colors, such as Harvard University Crimson or Syracuse University Orange.

31

Old-style Football Helmets

Back in 1951, football helmets were a lot different than they are today. They were smaller, and they had no face masks. Before 1939, college players weren't even required to wear helmets.

Helmets didn't exist when young American men started playing football about 150 years ago. Players would cover their heads and ears with bandanas or grow long hair to protect their heads. The first football helmet was a leather head-cover made in 1893 by a shoemaker for a player at the U.S. Naval Academy. That early helmet led the way to more substantial, padded leather helmets.

Early football helmets were brown and had no team or school symbol or any other

32

adornments. After the invention of the forward pass in 1906, it became advantageous for ball-catchers (*receivers*) to wear colored helmets so the quarterback could more readily see them downfield.

In 1939, the plastic football helmet was invented. Compared to leather helmets, plastic helmets are stronger, more durable, and lighter. Also, they have a web suspension inside so the helmet can be fit to a player's head. Eventually, chin straps and face masks were added to helmets. Football helmet makers continually improve helmet design, especially to protect the players from concussions and other serious head injuries.

Rushing

Rushing is running with the ball after it is hiked.

When American colleges began playing it around 1870, football was a version of rugby, a game invented in England in the 1830s. Then, in 1880, Yale University's football coach, Walter Camp, convinced other colleges to play by rules that he invented specifically for American football.

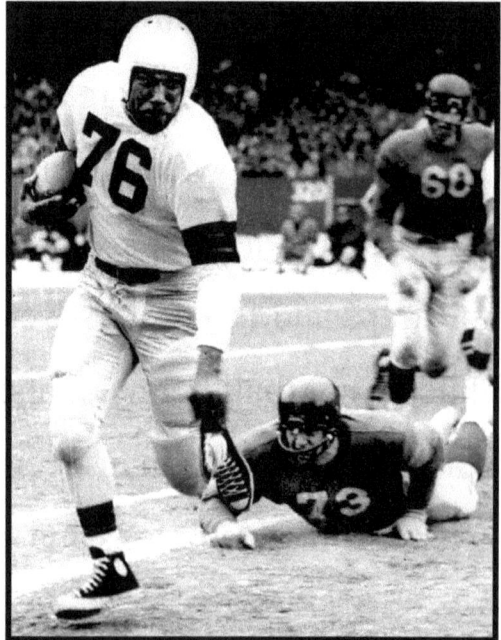

Some of these rules involved running with the ball. For example, in rugby (as in soccer), play rarely stops and there is no blocking. Coach Camp's rules changed that. He said that the team with the ball could have three chances (*downs*) to move the ball five yards (that changed to 10 yards in 1906; a fourth down was added in 1912). A ball carrier could be behind blockers on a seven-man scrimmage line, and teams could plan different strategies for moving the ball (*plays*). Each play started with a center giving (*hiking*) the ball to a quarterback when signaled to do so. The quarterback could run with the ball, give it (*hand off*) to another player to run with, or throw it (*pass*) to a teammate.

The Heisman Trophy

The Heisman Trophy is awarded to the best American college football player of the year. The winner is chosen by a group consisting of 870 American sports writers and broadcasters, every former Heisman Trophy winner, and one fan.

The trophy is a bronze statue of a muscular football player driving forward with the ball. It is 14 inches long, 13 inches high, and weighs 25 pounds. It is named for John W. Heisman, who coached at several colleges. Heisman became athletic director of the Downtown Athletic Club of New York City and invented the voting system used to choose the winner of the award that now carries his name.

The NFL Hall of Fame

The National Football League (NFL) honors individuals who have made the greatest contributions to football by selecting them to be in the Hall of Fame. About 250 individuals are members of the NFL Hall of Fame. They include outstanding players, coaches, football journalists, football broadcasters, and team executives.

The Hall of Fame is in located in Canton, Ohio. On display are statues of Hall-of-Famers and professional football's historic documents and artifacts. Each year thousands of people visit the NLF Hall of Fame.

African-Americans in College Football

African-American students have played
football at American colleges
since the game's beginnings
between 1865 and 1880. The first
African-American All America
was William Henry Lewis, who
played center for Amherst

William Henry Lewis

College in 1889. Lewis went on to Harvard Law

**Paul Le Roy
Robeson**

School and played football there.

Paul Le Roy Robeson was
an exceptional lineman for
Rutgers University. He was All-
America in 1917 and 1918. Yale
coach Walter Camp said Robeson
"was the finest end that ever
played the game, college or
professional." In 1916, Robeson
was held out of a game because the opposing team

38

refused to compete against African-American players. Robeson was the top student in his college graduating class. After college, Robeson played professional football in order to pay tuition at Columbia Law School. Robeson became a famous opera singer, actor, and outspoken champion for African-American rights and equality.

Frederick Douglass "Fritz" Pollard was an All-America running back at Brown University. In 1915, he became the first African-American to play in a Rose Bowl game. In 1916, he broke the world record in the low hurdles and qualified for the U.S. Olympic Team.

"Fritz" Pollard

In 1920, he became a professional football player and in 1922 the first African-American professional football coach.

Making Money in Professional Sports

College football players are not allowed to be paid to play their sport. Only professional football players can be paid.

Nine members of the 1951 University of San Francisco Dons football team went on to play professional football. Back then, professional football players earned between $7000 and $10,000 a year, about the same as an engineer, a bit more than a teacher, and a lot less than a doctor. Players generally played for a few years and then found other work to support themselves and their families.

Today, it's a lot different. The average pay for an American professional football player is about $1 million a year. Some players earn more than $10 million a year. The highest paid players earn over $20 million a year. A million dollars a year would pay for seven doctors, or 15 police officers, or 20 teachers, or 20,000 school books, or 2 million white-board markers. A professional football player will earn more money playing football in two years than a teacher will for teaching for 20 years.

Top 5 NFL salaries of 2009 as reported by USA Today

1	Philip Rivers	$25,556,630
2.	Jay Cutler	$22,044,090
3.	Eli Manning	$20,500,000
4.	Kurt Warner	$19,004,680
5.	Kelvin Hayden	$17,480,000

College Students and Racial Equality

The players on the 1951 University of San Francisco football team were among many American college students who challenged racial segregation in the southern part of the United States during the 1950s and 1960s.

In 1960, four African-American college students in Greensboro, North Carolina, sat at a segregated lunch counter reserved for white people. The students were refused service but they stayed in their seats. "We believe, since we buy books and papers in the other part of the store, we should get served in this part," they said.

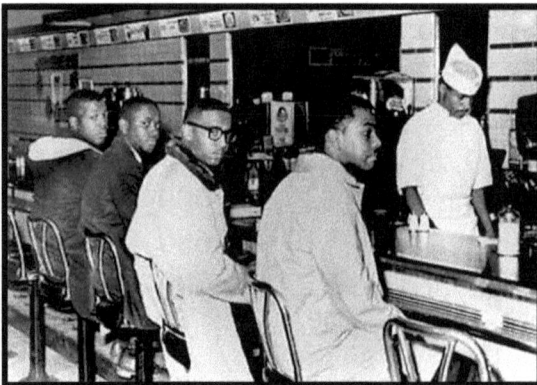

In 1960, students from North Carolina Agricultural and Technical College refused to leave a store lunch counter in Greensboro, North Carolina.

This was the first of many similar nonviolent "sit-ins" in the south. About 70,000 people from all over America participated in sit-ins; 3000 were arrested for breaking local laws.

In 1961, more than 1000 African-American and white college students from all over America took bus trips through the southeastern United States to test new U.S. laws that prohibited segregation in interstate travel facilities, including bus and railway stations. These students were called "freedom riders." They were attacked by angry mobs along the way.

1964, the U.S. Congress passed the Civil Rights Act declaring discrimination based on race illegal.

References

Clark, Kristine S. (2003). *Undefeated, Untied, and Uninvited: A Documentary of the 1951 University of San Francisco Dons Football Team.* Santa Ana, CA: Griffin Publishing.

Garcia, Ken (2000, July 8). Giving '51 Dons Their Due: Presidential apology asked to atone for racist snub that kept greatest USF football team from bowl games. *San Francisco Chronicle.*

Newhouse, D. (2006, December 26). Stand against racism hallmark of '51 team. *Oakland Tribune.*

Nolte, Carl (2006, May 20). Honoring integrity: USF's last football team refused to compromise. *San Francisco Chronicle.*

Perrin, Tom (1987). *Football: A College History.* Jefferson, NC: McFarland & Company.

Watterson, John S (2000). *College Football.* Baltimore: Johns Hopkins University Press.

Photo Credits

Front cover: Courtesy of the University of San Francisco

Page 5: Courtesy of the University of San Francisco

Page 6: Courtesy of the University of San Francisco

Page 8: Courtesy of the University of San Francisco

Page 12: Courtesy of the City of Miami

Page 14: Courtesy of the University of San Francisco

Page 19: Library of Congress Prints and Photographs Division

Page 20: Library of Congress Prints and Photographs Division

Page 21: Courtesy of the United States Air Force (020903-o-9999b-098.jpg)

Page 22: Bill Willis and Marion Motley, Associated Press

Page 23: Associated Press Photo

Page 24: CORBIS

Page 25: Chris Trotman, Getty Images

Page 27: Paul Chinn/San Francisco Chronicle

Page 29: Library of Congress Prints and Photographs Division

Page 30: Library of Congress Prints and Photographs Division

Page 31: Courtesy of the University of San Francisco

Page 32: Courtesy of the University of San Francisco

Page 34: Associated Press

Page 36: Courtesy of Destination360 (http://www.destination360.com)

Page 38: William Henry Lewis courtesy of Harvard University Digital Image Archives

Page 38: Paul Robeson courtesy of The Paul Robeson Cultural Center, Rutgers, The State University of New Jersey.

Page 39: Courtesy of Brown University Library

Page 42: Library of Congress Prints and Photographs Division

Photo Credits

www.ingramcontent.com/pod-product-compliance
Lightning Source LLC
Chambersburg PA
CBHW060632030426
42337CB00018B/3313